ALTERNATOR BOOKS™

THE MANHATTAN PROJECT

Matt Doeden

Lerner Publications ◆ Minneapolis

Lerner Publications Company
A division of Lerner Publishing Group, Inc.
241 First Avenue North
Minneapolis, MN 55401 USA

For reading levels and more information, look up this title at www.lernerbooks.com.

Main body text set in Aptifer Slab LT Pro Regular 11.5/18.
Typeface provided by Linotype AG.

Library of Congress Cataloging-in-Publication Data

Names: Doeden, Matt, author.
Title: The Manhattan Project / Matt Doeden.
Description: Minneapolis : Lerner Publications, [2017] | Series: Heroes
    of World War II | Audience: Ages 8–12. | Audience: Grades 4 to 6. |
    Includes bibliographical references and index.
Identifiers: LCCN 2017044242 (print) | LCCN 2017050383 (ebook) |
    ISBN 9781541521582 (eb pdf) | ISBN 9781541521506 (lb : alk. paper)
Subjects: LCSH: Manhattan Project (U.S.)—Juvenile literature. | Atomic
    bomb—United States—History—Juvenile literature. | Military
    weapons—History—20th century—Juvenile literature. | World War,
    1939–1945—Juvenile literature.
Classification: LCC QC773.3.U5 (ebook) | LCC QC773.3.U5 D64 2017
    (print) | DDC 355.8/25119/0973—dc23

LC record available at https://lccn.loc.gov/2017044242

Manufactured in the United States of America
1-44379-34644-12/20/2017

CONTENTS

INTRODUCTION
LITTLE BOY

US colonel Paul W. Tibbets peered through a window of the **B-29 Superfortress** *Enola Gay*. Far below him lay the Pacific Ocean. Ahead, he could see a dark mass in the ocean. Japan was in sight.

Enola Gay was one of thousands of B-29 Superfortress airplanes used during World War II (1939–1945).

It was the morning of August 6, 1945. The United States had flown countless bombing missions over Japan in recent months. But this one was different. The *Enola Gay* carried a bomb designed to end World War II.

Paul W. Tibbets

The bomb was the creation of the top-secret Manhattan Project. Scientists with the project had been tasked with developing a new weapon of incredible power—an atomic bomb, also called a nuclear bomb. For the first time, the US military was about to use it.

Tibbets was the commander of the mission. He guided the plane over the Japanese city of Hiroshima. Major Thomas Ferebee, the mission's **bombardier**, released a 9,700-pound (4,400 kg) bomb called Little Boy.

Deep within the bomb lay **uranium-235 (U-235)**. The uranium underwent **fission**. In an instant, the bomb released energy equal to about 15,000 tons (13,608 t) of **TNT**.

A thick, mushroom-shaped cloud of smoke rose into the air over Hiroshima. The explosion engulfed the city in a massive fireball. Buildings crumbled. About eighty thousand people died instantly. Thousands more would die in the years that followed. Three days later, the United States dropped an atomic bomb called Fat Man on the Japanese city of Nagasaki.

STEM HIGHLIGHT

Fission is a process that splits certain atoms, such as uranium. When they split, the atoms shed particles called neutrons, along with huge amounts of energy.

The released neutrons may strike other atoms, causing them to split. This starts a **chain reaction**. More atoms split, releasing more atom-splitting neutrons and energy. The result is an explosion of terrible power.

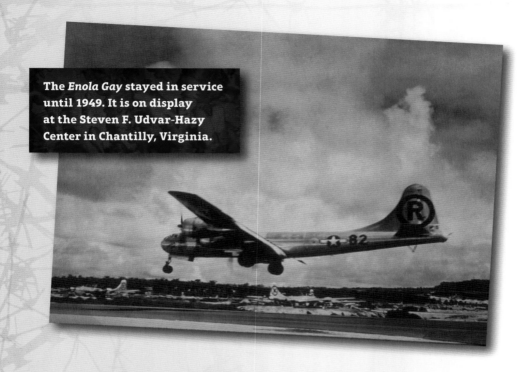

Captain Robert Lewis, copilot of the *Enola Gay*, turned away from the scene at Hiroshima. He was overcome by emotion. Lewis scribbled into his journal, "My god, what have we done?"

World War II began in 1939 when Germany invaded Poland. Germany, Italy, Japan, and other nations formed the Axis powers. Britain and France declared war on Germany in 1939. Along with the United States and other countries, they became the Allied powers. Before long, the United States started the Manhattan Project with the goal of ending the war.

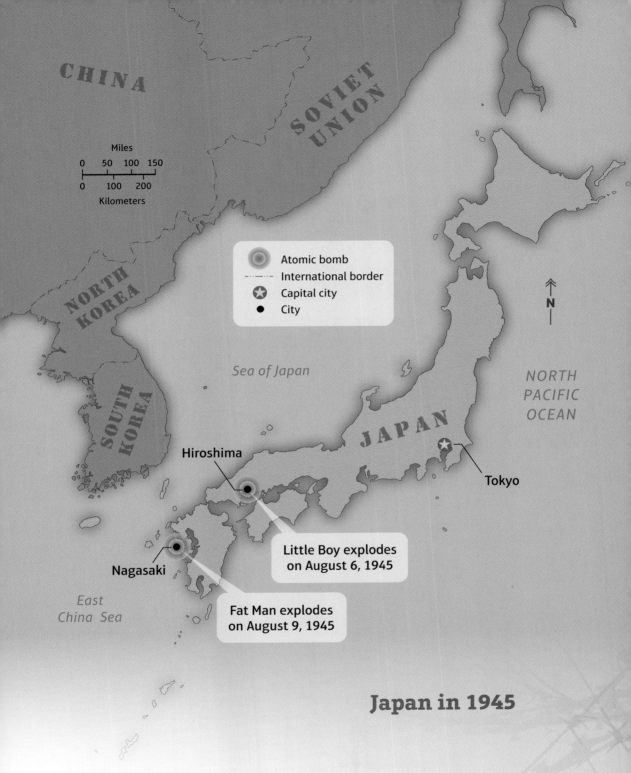

Miles
0 50 100 150

0 100 200
Kilometers

CHINA

SOVIET UNION

NORTH KOREA

SOUTH KOREA

Sea of Japan

JAPAN

NORTH PACIFIC OCEAN

N

Atomic bomb
International border
Capital city
City

Hiroshima

Tokyo

Nagasaki

Little Boy explodes on August 6, 1945

Fat Man explodes on August 9, 1945

East China Sea

Japan in 1945

CHAPTER 1
THE ORIGINS OF THE MANHATTAN PROJECT

Physicist Leo Szilard was on the leading edge of nuclear research in the late 1930s. As World War II began, few people could grasp the power of atomic weapons. But Szilard understood. An atomic bomb could make the Axis powers unstoppable. He wanted to make sure that didn't happen.

German troops post a sign on a store owned by Jewish people in 1933. The Nazi German government killed about six million Jews during World War II.

Leo Szilard

The United States had not yet entered the war. But in August 1939, Szilard wrote a letter to US president Franklin D. Roosevelt. The letter urged the United States to begin a nuclear program. And it warned that Germany's efforts to build a bomb might already be under way. The world's most famous physicist, Albert Einstein, signed the letter.

Roosevelt took the warning seriously. He knew the United States had to build an atomic bomb before Germany did. The Manhattan Project soon began.

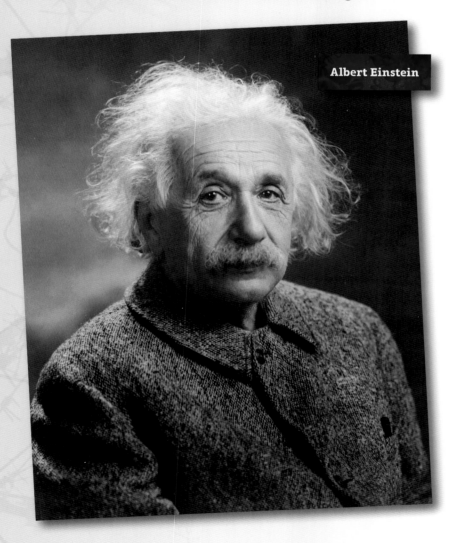

Albert Einstein

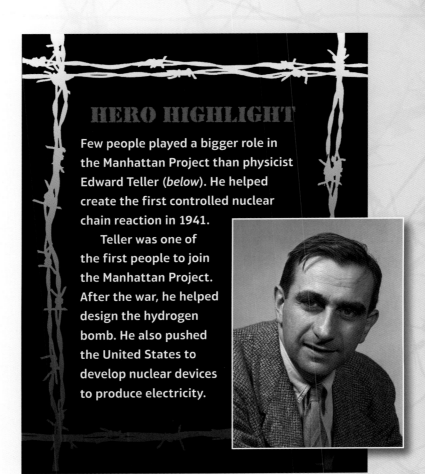

HERO HIGHLIGHT

Few people played a bigger role in the Manhattan Project than physicist Edward Teller (*below*). He helped create the first controlled nuclear chain reaction in 1941.

Teller was one of the first people to join the Manhattan Project. After the war, he helped design the hydrogen bomb. He also pushed the United States to develop nuclear devices to produce electricity.

CHAPTER 2
BUILDING THE BOMBS

The heart of the Manhattan Project was at Los Alamos, New Mexico. The Los Alamos National Laboratory opened in 1943. The lab grew into a small city with thousands of people working on designs for an atomic bomb. Yet somehow, it remained a secret.

Scientists such as J. Robert Oppenheimer (*left*) became famous for their work on the Manhattan Project.

The Manhattan Project was more than just one project. Teams of scientists worked with a range of different bomb designs. Some used U-235. Others used the element **plutonium**. No one knew for sure what design or element was going to work.

THE SECRET SITE

To use uranium for a bomb, the scientists at Los Alamos needed U-235. This type, or **isotope**, of uranium is capable of a chain reaction. However, U-235 made up a tiny portion of the uranium mined at the time. Scientists needed to enrich, or separate, the U-235 from other uranium isotopes.

A site called Oak Ridge in Tennessee became the center of the enrichment effort in 1942. Up to thirty thousand people worked at the site. Chemist William Ginell was one of them. Potential workers were kept in the dark about the project until they were hired. "[The job interviewer] couldn't tell me what [the job] was or where it was or anything about it," he said.

In 1945 Oak Ridge achieved its goal. It had enriched enough U-235 for an atomic bomb. Years of work and tens of thousands of people had done the job.

THE PLUTONIUM PATH

On December 2, 1942, physicist George Weil stood in a basement at the University of Chicago. Before him stood Chicago Pile-1 (CP-1), the world's first **nuclear**

Chicago Pile-1 looked like a big pile of bricks. Together, the bricks weighed more than 700,000 pounds (317,515 kg).

reactor. He and his team were about to change nuclear science and the Manhattan Project forever.

In 1940 scientists had discovered a new element, plutonium. Like U-235, plutonium could fuel a nuclear chain reaction. Plutonium could also be made in a lab.

Physicists create plutonium by causing uranium to absorb neutrons. The process requires a nuclear reactor. So that's what physicist Enrico Fermi's team helped build in Chicago. They used rods to control the reactor. The rods absorbed neutrons and prevented them from splitting atoms, which would cause a chain reaction.

Weil's job was simple. He carefully pulled the final control rod out of CP-1. Nothing remained to stop a chain reaction.

Nearby, the team's instruments began to click faster and faster. The instruments were counting neutrons. The clicks showed that nuclear fission was beginning. The team carefully controlled the reaction with rods and other safety measures. With the working CP-1 reactor, the Manhattan Project had a new bomb-fuel option.

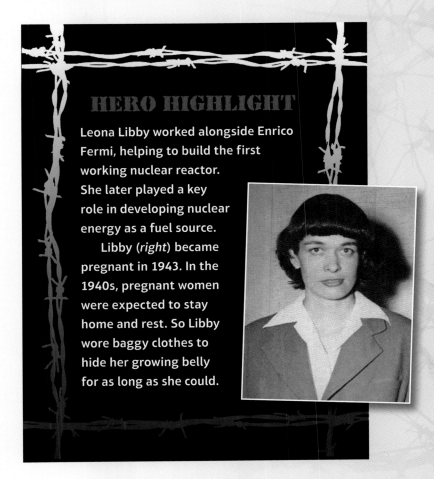

HERO HIGHLIGHT

Leona Libby worked alongside Enrico Fermi, helping to build the first working nuclear reactor. She later played a key role in developing nuclear energy as a fuel source.

Libby (*right*) became pregnant in 1943. In the 1940s, pregnant women were expected to stay home and rest. So Libby wore baggy clothes to hide her growing belly for as long as she could.

CHAPTER 3
TRINITY

By June 1945, the Manhattan Project had finally collected enough U-235 to make a single bomb. With just one, there was no way to test the bomb before using it.

Workers prepare the world's first atomic bomb test at Trinity Site in 1945.

Plutonium could be made in a reactor faster than U-235 could be enriched, so the United States had enough plutonium for more than one bomb. On July 16, 1945, scientists and military officials gathered in the New Mexico desert at Trinity Site. They intended to test the world's first atomic bomb.

A NEW DAWN

A steel tower stood above Trinity Site early that morning. At the top of the tower sat a metal object—the bomb.

Miles away, at a control bunker, tensions ran high. Physicist Edward Teller feared the power of the bomb would put the team at risk. He passed sunblock around, warning that everyone could be bathed in a blast of harmful **radiation**.

STEM HIGHLIGHT

The plutonium bomb developed by the Manhattan Project was a large metal sphere. The plutonium lay at the bomb's core. Surrounding the core was a series of explosive charges.

To **detonate** the bomb, the charges were fired at the same time. The explosive force rushed inward. The force compacted the plutonium, causing fission to begin.

At another site nearby, General Leslie Groves worried that the bomb wouldn't work. Groves had devoted years to the project. He wrote, "I thought only of what I would do if the countdown got to zero and nothing happened."

Three . . . two . . . one . . .

An intense blast lit up the landscape. A glowing fireball rose high into the sky. The steel tower became vapor, and a powerful **shock wave** ripped across the desert. The force of the bomb was much greater than scientists had estimated.

The nuclear age had begun.

The site of the world's first nuclear explosion is a US national park called White Sands National Monument.

Harry Truman (*left*) became president of the United States when Franklin Roosevelt died in 1945.

TRUMAN'S DECISION

The war in Europe ended in defeat for the Axis in the spring of 1945. US president Harry Truman and the Allied powers turned their focus to Japan. Allied leaders feared that only an invasion of Japan would force the country's surrender. Such a plan would cost the lives of countless people on both sides.

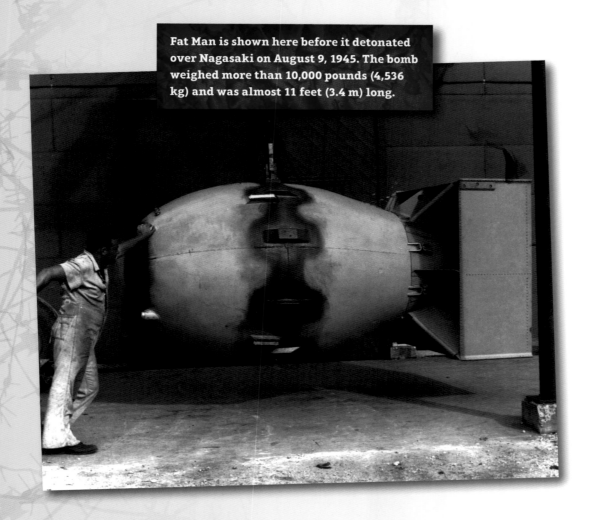

Fat Man is shown here before it detonated over Nagasaki on August 9, 1945. The bomb weighed more than 10,000 pounds (4,536 kg) and was almost 11 feet (3.4 m) long.

The successful test at Trinity Site gave Truman a new option. He had been president for only a few months. He hadn't even known of the Manhattan Project before April 1945. But he had to decide how to use the project's destructive new weapon.

On July 26, 1945, Truman and other world leaders demanded Japan's surrender. The Japanese government refused. So Truman gave the order. He told the US Army Air Forces to drop atomic bombs on Japan. On August 6 and August 9, the army fulfilled Truman's order.

Between forty thousand and seventy-five thousand people were killed instantly when Fat Man detonated above Nagasaki on August 9.

CHAPTER 4
AFTER THE BOMBS

The bombings of Hiroshima and Nagasaki ended Japan's
will to fight. On August 14, 1945, Japan announced its
surrender. World War II was over.

For many, the use of two atomic bombs was cause
for celebration. Years of work and billions of dollars
had helped end a bloody war. The Allies had avoided a
costly invasion of Japan.

President Truman announces Japan's
surrender to reporters on August 14, 1945.
The date became known as V-J Day, or
Victory over Japan Day.

Yet as people reviewed accounts and photos of the destruction, it became clear that Japan suffered terribly from the bombings. The two bombs immediately killed more than one hundred thousand people. Many more suffered and died later from lack of food and water, burns, and sickness.

Several scientists regretted their roles in the Manhattan Project. Physicist Mark Oliphant was crippled with grief. He described himself as a war criminal.

In October 1945, J. Robert Oppenheimer, the lead scientist on the Manhattan Project, visited Truman. "Mr. President, I feel I have blood on my hands," he said. Oppenheimer wasn't talking about the victims in Japan. He was concerned that atomic weapons would be used again to cause even more destruction.

Some people have called J. Robert Oppenheimer the father of the atomic bomb.

Would invading Japan have resulted in fewer deaths than dropping the bombs? Would a demonstration of an atomic bomb in a remote area have caused Japan to surrender? There are no easy answers. One thing is certain, however. The Manhattan Project succeeded in ending World War II.

The Hiroshima Peace Memorial Park reminds people of the incredible destructive power of atomic weapons.

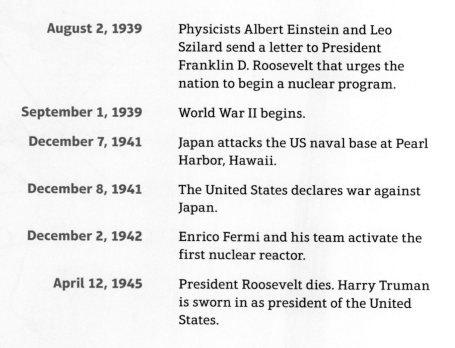

August 2, 1939	Physicists Albert Einstein and Leo Szilard send a letter to President Franklin D. Roosevelt that urges the nation to begin a nuclear program.
September 1, 1939	World War II begins.
December 7, 1941	Japan attacks the US naval base at Pearl Harbor, Hawaii.
December 8, 1941	The United States declares war against Japan.
December 2, 1942	Enrico Fermi and his team activate the first nuclear reactor.
April 12, 1945	President Roosevelt dies. Harry Truman is sworn in as president of the United States.

May 8, 1945	The war in Europe ends with Germany's surrender. Allied efforts focus on Japan.
July 16, 1945	The first controlled atomic explosion takes place at Trinity Site. The nuclear age begins.
August 6, 1945	Little Boy, a U-235 bomb, detonates over Hiroshima.
August 9, 1945	Fat Man, a plutonium bomb, detonates over Nagasaki.
August 14, 1945	Japan announces its surrender, ending World War II.

Source Notes

8 "My God . . . What Have We Done?," *Newsweek*, July 23, 1995, http://www.newsweek.com/my-god-what-have-we-done-184696.

15 "William Ginell's Interview," Voices of the Manhattan Project, February 22, 2017, http://manhattanprojectvoices.org/oral-histories/william-ginells-interview.

20 "The Trinity Test," US Department of Energy, accessed September 21, 2017, https://www.osti.gov/opennet/manhattan-project-history/Events/1945/trinity.htm.

26 Paul Ham, "As Hiroshima Smouldered, Our Atom Bomb Scientists Suffered Remorse," *Newsweek*, August 5, 2015, http://www.newsweek.com/hiroshima-smouldered-our-atom-bomb-scientists-suffered-remorse-360125.

Glossary

bombardier: an airplane crew member whose job is to release bombs

B-29 Superfortress: a long-range airplane designed to drop bombs

chain reaction: a series of events with each event causing the next one

detonate: cause to explode

fission: the splitting of an atom's nucleus, resulting in a release of energy

isotope: an element that contains a different number of neutrons from other forms of that element

nuclear reactor: a device capable of producing energy and material from a controlled nuclear reaction

plutonium: an element made by people and used in fission

radiation: waves of energy

shock wave: a powerful burst of air and energy from an explosion

TNT: a substance used as a high explosive

uranium-235 (U-235): an isotope of uranium that is used in fission

FURTHER INFORMATION

Baxter, Roberta. *The Dropping of the Atomic Bombs*. Ann Arbor, MI: Cherry Lake, 2014.

Bodden, Valerie. *Nuclear Physicist Chien-Shiung Wu*. Minneapolis: Lerner Publications, 2017.

Ducksters: World War II
http://www.ducksters.com/history/world_war_ii

How Nuclear Bombs Work: Nuclear Fission
http://science.howstuffworks.com/nuclear-bomb2.htm

Manhattan Project
http://www.american-historama.org/1929-1945-depression-ww2-era/manhattan-project.htm

Ripley, Tim. *Torpedoes, Missiles, and Cannons: Physics Goes to War*. Minneapolis: Lerner Publications, 2018.

Stelson, Caren. *Sachiko: A Nagasaki Bomb Survivor's Story*. Minneapolis: Carolrhoda Books, 2016.

Index

Photo Acknowledgments

The images in this book are used with the permission of: © iStockphoto.
com/akinshin (barbed wire background); Universal History Archive/UIG/
Getty Images, pp. 4–5; United States Air Force/Wikimedia Commons (public
domain), p. 6; Universal Images Group/Getty Images, pp. 7, 29 (left); John
van Hasselt/Sygma/Getty Images, pp. 8, 29 (right); © Laura Westlund/
Independent Picture Service, p. 9; ullstein bild/Getty Images, p. 10;
PhotoQuest/Archive Photos/Getty Images, p. 11; Library of Congress pp. 12
(LC-USZ62-60242), 21 (LC-USZ62-117122); Corbis/Getty Images, pp. 13, 18, 20,
24, 28; Bettmann/Getty Images, pp. 14, 26; Wikimedia Commons (public
domain), pp. 16, 17; Time Life Pictures/National Archives/The LIFE Picture
Collection/Getty Images, pp. 22, 25; Prisma Bildagentur/UIG/Getty Images,
p. 23; Cultura/Getty Images, p. 27.

Front cover: National Archives (bomb); © iStockphoto.com/akinshin (barbed
wire background); © iStockphoto.com/ElementalImaging (camouflage
background); © iStockphoto.com/MillefloreImages (flag background).